TO: Lesley

To New Adventure

FROM: SI May

THE WISDOM OF OWLS

Published by Sellers Publishing, Inc.
161 John Roberts Road, South Portland, ME 04106
Visit us at www.sellerspublishing.com • E-mail: rsp@rsvp.com

 Like Us on Facebook

Compiled by Robin Haywood

ISBN-13: 978-1-4162-4538-4

Printed and bound in China.

10 9 8 7 6 5 4 3 2 1

THE WISDOM OF OWLS
GOOD ADVICE AS YOU TAKE FLIGHT

Art by Debbie Mumm

SELLERS
PUBLISHING

The next best thing
to being wise oneself
is to live in a circle of those who are.

—C. S. LEWIS

©Debbie Mumm

©Debbie Mumm

A good head and
a good heart are always
a formidable combination.

—Nelson Mandela

Your life is always under
construction. It is your job
to learn how to untangle
the threads and weave a tapestry
that matches your desires.

—DANNYE WILLIAMSEN

©Debbie Mumm.

Be soft. Do not let the world make you hard. Do not let bitterness steal your sweetness. Take pride that even though the rest of the world may disagree, you still believe it to be a beautiful place.

—KURT VONNEGUT

©Debbie Mumm

©Debbie Mumm

Be happy.
It's one way
of being wise.

—Sidonie Gabrielle Colette

©Debbie Mumm

If you don't feel it, flee from it.
Go where you are celebrated,
not merely tolerated.

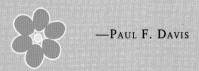 —PAUL F. DAVIS

In the long run, we shape our lives, and we shape ourselves. The process never ends until we die. And the choices we make are ultimately our own responsibility.

—Eleanor Roosevelt

©Debbie Mumm

©Debbie Mumm

Lucy: "You learn more when you lose. . . ."
Charlie Brown: "Well then, I must be the smartest person in the world!"

—CHARLES M. SCHULZ

©Debbie Mumm

The art of being wise is the art
of knowing what to overlook.

—WILLIAM JAMES

Sometimes, if you stand on the bottom rail of a bridge and lean over to watch the river slipping slowly away beneath you, you will suddenly know everything there is to be known.

—A. A. MILNE

©Debbie Mumm

©Debbie Mumm

"Life is a journey, Frannie darling,"
Feagan had once told me.
"Choose well those with whom
you travel."

—Lorraine Heath

©Debbie Mumm

Always keep an open mind
and a compassionate heart.

—PHIL JACKSON

We are what our thoughts have made us; so take care about what you think. Words are secondary. Thoughts live; they travel far.

—Swami Vivekananda

©Debbie Mumm

©Debbie Mumm

"It's a dangerous business, Frodo, going out your door. You step onto the road, and if you don't keep your feet, there's no knowing where you might be swept off to."

—J. R. R. TOLKIEN

©Debbie Mumm

Happiness isn't the reward we retrieve after a long struggle. It arrives daily, in those clear moments when our hearts are tender, pricked by the embrace of a loved one, the beauty of a single flower, the majesty of the world in which we are central.

—TONI SORENSON

©Debbie Mumm

When written in Chinese, the word "crisis" is composed of two characters. One represents danger and the other represents opportunity.

—JOHN F. KENNEDY

I have just three things to teach:
simplicity, patience, compassion.
These three are your greatest
treasures.

—Lao Tzu

©Debbie Mumm

©Debbie Mumm

Turn your wounds into wisdom.

—Oprah Winfrey

Sometimes your joy is the source of your smile, but sometimes your smile can be the source of your joy.

—Thích Nhất Hạnh

©Debbie Mumm

Wisdom is not wisdom when
it is derived from books alone.

—HORACE

©Debbie Mumm

©Debbie Mumm

We must be willing to let
go of the life we planned
so as to have the life that is
waiting for us.

—JOSEPH CAMPBELL

Once you make a decision,
the universe conspires to
make it happen.

—Ralph Waldo Emerson

© Debbie Mumm

©Debbie Mumm

Think before you speak.
Read before you think.

—FRAN LEBOWITZ

©Debbie Mumm

There are moments when troubles enter our lives and we can do nothing to avoid them. But they are there for a reason. Only when we have overcome them will we understand why they were there.

—Paulo Coelho

Do one thing every day
that scares you.

—Eleanor Roosevelt

©Debbie Mumm

Water is the softest thing, yet it can penetrate mountains and earth. This shows clearly the principle of softness overcoming hardness.

—LAO TZU

©Debbie Mumm

©Debbie Mumm

You have to do your own
growing no matter how
tall your grandfather was.

—ABRAHAM LINCOLN

How noble and good everyone could be if, every evening before falling asleep, they were to recall to mind the events of the whole day and consider exactly what has been good and bad. Then, without realizing it, you try to improve yourself at the start of each new day; of course, you achieve quite a lot in the course of time. Anyone can do this, it costs nothing and is certainly very helpful.

—ANNE FRANK

©Debbie Mumm

©Debbie Mumm

You have brains in your head.
You have feet in your shoes.
You can steer yourself in any
direction you choose.

—THEODOR SEUSS GEISEL (DR. SEUSS)

©Debbie Mumm

Yesterday I was clever,
so I wanted to change the world.
Today I am wise,
so I am changing myself.

—Rumi

CREDITS

p. 25 Lorraine Heath, *Surrender to the Devil*; p. 31, J. R. R. Tolkien, *The Lord of the Rings*; p. 49 Fran Lebowitz, *The Fran Lebowitz Reader*; p. 51 Paulo Coelho, *The Fifth Mountain*; p. 58 Anne Frank, *The Diary of Anne Frank, Revised Critical Edition*; p. 61 Theodor Seuss Geisel (Dr. Seuss), *Oh, the Places You'll Go!*